Original title:
Echoes of the Elm

Copyright © 2025 Creative Arts Management OÜ
All rights reserved.

Author: Juliette Kensington
ISBN HARDBACK: 978-1-80567-277-7
ISBN PAPERBACK: 978-1-80567-576-1

Where Time Wears Its Wisdom

In the park where old folks play,
Life's punchlines throw us off-balance,
Wrinkles laugh as time slips away,
At the end, we all share the silence.

Like squirrels with acorns in tow,
Chasing dreams of a grand buffet,
With every slip, there's a show,
As laughter dances, we sway.

Tranquility in the Twine

Beneath the branches, a wild vine,
Whispers jokes to the birds on high,
While the bees sip tea, feeling fine,
Clouds drift by with a wink and a sigh.

Twirling leaves with a sly little grin,
Where laughter rests on every bough,
The wind hums a tune made of whim,
And even the shadows laugh somehow.

The Gentle Caress of Age

A wise old branch, a laughter-filled tale,
Of clumsy teens who danced with fate,
   Forgotten tunes on a rusty pail,
   As the tree chuckles, never late.

With mossy hats, the squirrels convene,
For gossip floods in with each new breeze,
   In every wrinkle, there's humor seen,
   A tale that grows like ancient trees.

The Sound of Solitude

In the quiet, a chuckle takes flight,
As crickets play their nightly tunes,
One lonely owl, dressed up just right,
Grins at the moon, beneath which he swoons.

The silence bursts with a playful cheer,
As shadows jiggle, side by side,
In solitude, we hold what's dear,
Where every laugh and tear collide.

Hues of the Wind's Caress

Whispers in the air so bright,
A squirrel in a wig, what a sight!
Leaves dance like they lost a bet,
Trees giggle, you can't forget.

Branches stretch in playful tease,
A raccoon strums on rusty keys.
Sunbeams join the merry spree,
Nature's tune, a comedy.

The Chorus of the Forest Floor

A rabbit sings, it's off-key,
With a voice like a big ol' bee.
Frogs join in, a slimy band,
While crickets jam, a croaky hand.

Mushrooms sway, they steal the show,
In a concert of oddities, oh no!
Bunnies bounce in a glowing trance,
When to the beat, they prance and dance.

Beneath Green Canopies

Shadows giggle, light sneaks through,
A limbo line for ants in view.
Laughter spills from leafy crowns,
As branches sway in silly gowns.

Fungi sport a fancy poi,
While beetles bop, oh what a joy!
Each rustle brings a punchline new,
Life's a jest, from me to you.

Tales Laced in Twilight

As dusk creeps in, the fireflies glow,
A dance-off with a glowworm's show.
Owls debate, who knows the best,
In the art of wisebird jest.

Stars twinkle, casting witty pranks,
On wandering minds in playful flanks.
Every blink a brand-new cheer,
Night's humor, so bright and clear.

Virtues of the Verdant Canopy

Beneath the leafy arms so wide,
Squirrels play with acorns, a nutty pride.
Lovers kiss behind the trunk,
And giggles drift where shadows funk.

The branches twist like a curly fry,
Birds in suits like they're wondering why.
Nature's own comedians, don't you see?
Their punchlines flutter in the gentle spree.

Trees that Time Forgot

Once a wise oak stood so tall,
Now he tells jokes to a tree with a sprawl.
With bark so thick, he claims it's sweet,
While squirrels laugh, dodging his feet.

A pine cone fell with a clatter loud,
Landing right on a passing cloud.
"Oops!" said the cloud, "Don't drop it here!"
And the trees burst out in a fit of cheer.

Dialogues of the Dappled Light

Sunbeams dance like they've had too much,
While shadows play tag, oh what a touch!
A flicker here, a glimmer there,
Nature's light bounces to declare.

Moths gossip softly in the glow,
Whispering secrets from below.
The leaves are laughing, like they know why,
The sun asked the moon—'Are we too shy?'

Voices in the Breezy Stillness

The wind's a joker on a lazy spree,
Tickling the branches with glee.
Leaves rustle secrets, a comic relief,
As they gossip of life with newfound belief.

A twig interrupts, boasting a tale,
About a leaf who wanted to sail.
"You can float on a breeze!" said the wise old tree,
"But remember, dear friend, it's not for the free."

The Heartbeat of the Old Tree

In the shade where shadows play,
A squirrel sings his own ballet.
With acorns flying, leaves agree,
Nature's tune in harmony.

With every gust, the branches sway,
Tickling bark in a funny way.
A woodpecker drums on a trunk,
While deer prance round with a little funk.

The roots dig deep, a dance of sorts,
While rabbits race in playful jorts.
Mice tell tales of cheesy pies,
With every rustle, laughter flies.

So raise a toast to bark and leaves,
To whimsical wind that never grieves.
In laughter's arms, the day is free,
With every giggle from the tree.

Vibrations in the Whispers

The breeze carries tales, quite absurd,
Of a hedgehog who thinks he's a bird.
With wings made of cap and a smile so wide,
He tries to take off, it's quite a ride.

Beneath the canopy, shadows dart,
A rabbit races, oh, what a sport!
With every hop, he tales a chance,
Confusing a fox in a comical dance.

A parrot chimes in with a riddle,
While chipmunks play on a wooden fiddle.
Squirrels giggle as they plan their tricks,
Beneath the laughter of leafy flicks.

So listen close, the whispers ensue,
With every chuckle, the forest anew.
In playful prance, life spins around,
Nature's humor is always found.

The Lament of the Woodland

Oh, the trees sigh with a humorous tone,
For acorns thrown make them feel alone.
"Why not use leaves? They're much less dense!"
They grumble and mumble in their defense.

A sad raccoon looks for his stash,
For each dig in dirt, it's another crash.
His friends all laugh as he loses ground,
In this woodland, giggles always abound.

Birds gossip high, shaking their tails,
As they recount the shipwreck of snails.
"Such speed!" they chirp, but snails just smile,
Happy to know they'll win in a while.

So here in the woods, we mourn in glee,
Where laughter sprouts from the tallest tree.
In every sapling, a story's spun,
With every chuckle, we're having fun.

Carvings of Time

The old bark tells tales in grooves and knots,
Of the squirrels' games and the birds' silly thoughts.
With each carve of time, it chuckles benign,
As moss grows thick over each etched line.

A beaver sauntered, proud as can be,
With a tiny badge that says, "Look at me!"
Yet tripping on twigs, he falls with a splash,
Laughter erupts, a jovial bash.

Mushrooms dance in their odd little hats,
While frogs trade jests in acrobatic spats.
The sound of the stream is a comic refrain,
As laughter echoes back, again and again.

In shadows and light, the woodland plays,
A tapestry woven in whimsical ways.
With each passing season, the jokes stay prime,
The heart of nature carves joy into time.

The Memory of Leaves

Once a leaf tried to fly,
Stuck to a branch with a sigh.
A squirrel laughed and took aim,
Missed the target, what a game!

The wind whispered a joke,
As branches swayed and spoke.
A picnic of ants marched by,
Snacking on crumbs, oh my!

A tale spun in the breeze,
Rustling joke after joke with ease.
But the trees kept their secret tight,
Under the moon's soft light.

In autumn, the leaves fell down,
Dressed like clowns that lost their crown.
The ground wears laughter today,
In colors bright and gay!

Secrets in the Silhouette

In shadows where whispers dance,
The owls giggle at their chance.
A raccoon wearing a hat,
Winks at the moon, just like that!

The night is filled with delight,
As stars twinkle, oh what a sight.
Bushes tell stories unseen,
Of nights spent where they have been.

Patrols of ants dressed in black,
Marching on a mission, no slack.
They whispered, 'We rule this ground!'
While the crickets played around.

All creatures in jest, they play,
In the twilight, fading away.
With laughter echoing afar,
Beneath the night's strange star.

The Elder's Resonance

An elder tree with a grin,
Told jokes that made the woodpecker spin.
'Why did the twig cross the brook?'
It paused and nestled, then he took a look.

Raccoons gathered with glee,
Jesting all night under the tree.
A laugh erupted, so bold,
Of whispers shared, and tales retold.

At dawn, the fox came to boast,
'Last night's giggle? I had the most!'
The birds chirped in a chorus so sweet,
As laughter echoed through the street.

With branches wide, and leaves like fans,
It held the tales of silly plans.
The elder shook with every quip,
As nature danced on her friendship trip.

Murmurs in the Quiet Glade

In the glade where whispers tease,
A mossy log held a small breeze.
'What's the secret to your stay?'
'I nap all night, and work all day!'

Butterflies laughed in the sun,
Playing tag, it was all in fun.
The flowers blushed red and bright,
'We bloom just to tease their sight!'

A turtle pondered, so wise,
'Why rush when you can just disguise?'
The frogs in chorus croaked, 'You see,
We leap for joy, quite carelessly!'

The laughter filled the tranquil air,
With snippets of joy everywhere.
In that glade, life's sweet parade,
Each moment danced, none delayed.

The Breath of the Bowed Branches

In the breeze, they sway and dip,
Laughing leaves do a little flip.
Bowed branches tell a funny tale,
Of acorns doing a clumsy sail.

Squirrels prance, they take a chance,
Doing their dance, in leaf-filled pants.
A gust blows, and they lose their grip,
Down they tumble, a nutty trip!

The old tree sighs, a creaky joke,
As branches groove, like a hipster bloke.
Beneath the sun, they soak up cheer,
Sharing laughter, year after year.

With every rustle of their gown,
The tree roots giggle while it frowns.
In silence, laughter blooms and grows,
A wooden party, nature knows!

Roots in Stillness

Deep in the ground, they wiggle and squirm,
Roots in stillness, like a calm worm.
Under the soil, they plot mischief,
Watered with laughter, their only gift.

With every whisper of wind in the leaves,
They tell of pranks no one believes.
Dirt is the stage for the underground show,
Where roots can chuckle and giggle, oh no!

Stuck in the mud, they've found their groove,
Making mud pies, they never lose.
A tangle of fun and a twist of fate,
Rooty resilience, they celebrate!

From gnarled knots, they spin their tales,
In a steady voice that never fails.
These silent jesters, beneath the ground,
In stillness, a comedy can be found!

The Silence That Speaks

In quietude, the trees do stand,
With whispered jokes as they lend a hand.
A stoic bough with a knowing wink,
Makes squirrels giggle till they can't think.

The stillness hums a catchy tune,
As birds join in, beneath the moon.
A leaf flutters down with a mischievous grin,
Ready to join the playful din.

The shadows stretch, a comical sight,
As branches twist, oh what a fright!
A little breeze brings a burst of glee,
A silent jest from the wise old tree.

Laughter resonates in the quiet air,
Nature's humor everywhere.
In the silence, there's always a spark,
A funny story waiting in the dark!

Songs of the Seasoned Trees

Old trunks hum tunes of days gone by,
With melodies that make passersby cry.
Twisting tales in the autumn breeze,
These seasoned trees aim to please.

A warble here, a rustle there,
The bark begins a joyful flare.
"Knock, knock!" a squirrel sings with delight,
"Who's there?" croaks the owl, late at night.

With every ring, a laugh they share,
Tangled roots weaving tales with care.
In winter's grip or summer's charm,
Their stories dance and twine, so warm.

From acorn dreams to soaring high,
A tangled symphony, oh my, oh my!
Every leaf a note, a quirky theme,
Seasoned trees in their timeless dream!

Murmurs of the Forest Floor

Among the roots where critters dwell,
A squirrel's scheme goes very well.
He stashes nuts with quite a flair,
And laughs when others find it bare.

A raccoon sneaks with stealthy grace,
In search of snacks, he sets the pace.
A wiggle here, a tumble there,
Only to find a patch of hair!

Frogs croak jokes in croaky tones,
They leap and hop on mossy stones.
The toads all giggle, feeling spry,
While crickets chorus "Oh my, my!"

Beneath the ferns, the mushrooms grow,
They sway and dance, putting on a show.
With little hats, they wiggle free,
Quipped, "Who knew fungi could be so cheery?"

The Leafy Relic's Refrain

In foliage thick, where whispers cling,
The acorns drop, a dire thing.
Each thud a joke from nature's hand,
As squirrels scatter, it's quite unplanned.

The wise old owl dons specs of round,
With stories spun of sights profound.
"Remember kids, life's not a race,
Just keep your shades on, find your place!"

A playful breeze tugs at a vine,
It laughs and twirls, oh how divine!
Leaves chatter softly, plotting pranks,
As sunlight twinkles in leafy flanks.

Caterpillars take a slow, slow stroll,
While ants march in lines, playing their role.
They giggle as they carry their loads,
Managing snacks on winding roads.

The Ancient Timber's Tales

An ancient tree with bark so wise,
Tells tales that make the breezes rise.
"Back in my youth, oh what a sight,
I danced with storms all through the night!"

The woodpecker taps a syncopated beat,
"Your old yarns are cool, but mine can't be beat!
I've got the rhythm down to a T,
As I drum on your trunk, just wait and see!"

Little bugs parade in quirky lines,
With tiny hats and bright designs.
They gossip gossip, giggle and cheer,
Even the dew drops are drawn near.

Branches sway as if to say,
"Join our party, come and play!
With laughter sprouting from every curl,
This is the place where joy might unfurl."

The Whispering Canopy

Up in the boughs where secrets gleam,
Birds chirp tunes that dance like a dream.
They flit and flutter, under bright sky,
Yet pause just to giggle, oh my, oh my!

The wind whispers jokes from the past,
While hanging vines sway and contrast.
"Why don't trees use online chat?
Because they can't find any 'branch' to chat!"

Dappled light sprouts like jolly sprites,
Chasing shadows in playful flights.
The canopy chuckles, a tickled leaf,
Breezy banter, without a grief.

A curious squirrel scurries up high,
With acorns hidden, oh my, oh my.
He winks at the breeze and gives a shout,
"Let's keep this fun tree party about!"

Woodland Reveries

Beneath the leafy green,
Squirrels plot their schemes,
Whispering to the breeze,
As if sharing wild dreams.

Frogs croak their loud tunes,
With quite the funny flair,
While rabbits hop and dance,
Without a single care.

The trees lean down to listen,
To secrets softly told,
As acorns fall like laughter,
In the sunlight bright and bold.

With every rustling leaf,
A giggle takes its flight,
In the merry woodland realm,
Where day gives way to night.

Emotions Entwined in Vines

Vines twist in silly knots,
Creating quite a scene,
Flowers raise their petals,
In a laugh so keen.

Boys and girls run around,
With faces painted bright,
Chasing shadows of the trees,
In a playful, sweet delight.

A raccoon steals the picnic,
In a heist of pure delight,
While everyone just shrieks and gasps,
What a hilarious sight!

Laughter bounces through the air,
As sunlight starts to fade,
In a world where love and fun,
Are perfectly displayed.

The Subtle Art of Silence

In the calmest glades, we sit,
With nothing much to say,
Just listening to the quiet,
As animals make their play.

A lone owl hoots a joke,
That leaves the trees in fits,
While mushrooms giggle softly,
At the squirrel's silly skits.

Crickets chirp in rhythm,
With a beat that's quite absurd,
As they collaborate with frogs,
In concert, it's unheard!

Silence isn't empty here,
It's filled with giggles light,
In the gentle whispers shared,
Of woodland's sheer delight.

Fragments of Forgotten Stories

Once there was a badger,
Who thought he could take flight,
He climbed up on a toadstool,
And aimed for the moonlight.

Tales of brave adventures,
Spoken in jumbled tones,
As owls crack up in laughter,
From their lofty, ancient thrones.

A turtle wears a costume,
With a cape of leafy greens,
Dashing through the underbrush,
In his quirky, playful dreams.

Let's gather all these stories,
And share them with a cheer,
For in the woods, there's magic,
And laughter always near.

The Quivering Leaves' Confidentiality

In the shade where whispers roam,
Leaves gossip, hiding from home.
"Did you see that squirrel's dance?"
"He needs to give his nuts a chance!"

Branches wiggle, sharing jokes,
With cross-eyed critters, funny folks.
"Seagulls tried to steal my hat,"
"Too bad they only wear a mat!"

The acorns roll, they laugh and squeak,
"Your wig's a nutty, funny peak!"
Quivering leaves hold secrets tight,
Of whispered giggles day and night.

They peek at the world, all aglow,
With stories fast and laughs to throw.
It's a leafy, playful, mismatched crew,
Hiding laughs till the morning dew!

Echos in the Rustling Grass

Grass blades tickle, wave in glee,
"Who's that hopping? Oh, look, it's me!"
Worms squirm below, whisper in jest,
"I'm the wiggle champion, no need to test!"

Breezy whispers float on high,
As butterflies flutter, oh my, oh my!
"Did you see my last grand spin?"
"Oh yes, it was a whirly win!"

Frogs croak loud, with a punchline shout,
"Why did the chicken jump about?"
With each rustle, a giggling sound,
Nature's joke shop all around.

What a scene, under skies so bright,
With laughter hidden in plain sight.
Each rustle brings a quirky jest,
Where nature's humor shines the best!

The Timbered Tale

Once a tree with a trunk so grand,
Told tales of squirrels that were unplanned.
"Did I mention the one that stole,
My acorns, now he thinks he's whole?"

With bark like armor, he stood so proud,
Cackling laughter, he drew a crowd.
"Why would you wear a woodpecker's shoe?"
"Because my toe is full of goo!"

Branches waved like arms in cheer,
Telling secrets, loud and clear.
"Watch out for that raccoon thief,
He'll steal your snacks, he brings such grief!"

Each knot held stories, silly and bright,
Of frolicsome friends and magical flight.
With every creak, they'd spin a yarn,
Under the moonlight, none could be forlorn!

The Gentle Breeze's Confessions

The breeze sighed soft, with tales to share,
"Did you know about that jumpy hare?"
"I gave him a gust, off he flew,
Right into the pond, with a splish and a brew!"

With a tickle that swept through the park,
It carried scents, some sweet, some stark.
"Is that a sandwich in the air?"
"Oh please, keep that, it's my fair share!"

A dance with dandelions, cheeky and bold,
Whisking their seeds, a sight to behold.
"Why do flowers take so long to sneeze?"
"Because they enjoy the buzzing bees!"

The gentle breeze swirled round and round,
Discovering secrets, laughter unbound.
With every swoosh, it gave a grin,
Collecting chuckles from deep within!

Reverberations of Green

In a shady nook, squirrels play,
Chasing shadows throughout the day.
They trip on roots, stumble and twirl,
Beneath the leaves, they dance and whirl.

Laughter resonates, it's quite a show,
While ants march in line, just to and fro.
A chipmunk yells, "Watch where you tread!"
As grasshoppers leap from leaf to bed.

Beneath the boughs, the laughter grows,
With giggles and whispers, nature knows.
The world's a stage, with roles to assume,
Where dandelions burst forth to bloom.

So let's embrace what's silly and green,
In this leafy realm, life's never routine!
With nature's quirks, let us all unite,
For who can resist this woodland delight?

The Guardian's Lullaby

The old tree nods, its branches sway,
Murmering secrets from yesterday.
It chuckles softly, with much to share,
Of acorn adventures and windswept hair.

A wise owl hoots, perched high and snug,
While beetles dance a silly little rug.
They misconstrue the moon's bright face,
With wobbly steps in a nighttime race.

The breeze brings whispers, a playful tease,
As leaves are tickled by a gentle breeze.
Laughter echoes; it fills the night,
With giggles of critters in pure delight.

It guards the stories we all have told,
Where humor and warmth never grow cold.
In this cozy nook, the night's alive,
Among the chuckles, the old trees thrive.

Canopies of Time

Under the arch of twisting vines,
The tree's a jester, performing signs.
It bends with laughter, a crook in its back,
As time meanders like a lost track.

A butterfly flutters, clutching a joke,
Tickling a snail till it nearly broke.
With beetles laughing and crickets who sing,
It's a comedy show, and they're the king.

Each year adds a ring, each laugh a delight,
As the sun sets low, painting the night.
Whispers of joy in the morning dew,
In this lively realm, where all are true.

So dance under branches, embrace the fun,
With humor and joy, till the day is done.
Together we'll savor these moments divine,
In the playful heart of the forest's design.

Embracing the Old and Worn

The branches are tangled, the bark all frail,
With stories of mischief in every detail.
A wobbling squirrel with dreams too bold,
Stops for a laugh, while the stories unfold.

Leaves whisper giggles, a light-hearted cheer,
As rabbits bounce past without any fear.
Each gnarly knot shares a tale of the past,
As critters with laughter move quick and fast.

The world spins 'round amidst snickers and glee,
Every bump and twist, a part of the spree.
Embracing the wrinkled and aging with zest,
In the heart of the forest, we find our best.

So let's not disdain the old and the wise,
For humor resides in their lovable guise.
In the dance of the green, where we laugh and play,
We find that the worn leads to joy every day.

Sighs of the Woodland

In the grove, a squirrel pranced,
Chasing shadows, he danced.
A raccoon, with a cheeky grin,
Snatched the acorn, tossed it in!

The owl hooted, quite confused,
'Why can't these critters be bemused?'
The fox laughed, 'Oh what a mess!'
Leaves falling down, oh such finesse!

Beneath the shade, the rabbits play,
Digging tunnels, hop and sway.
While the bees hum tunes so sweet,
A flower says, 'You can't be beat!'

Whispers swirl with giggles bright,
Even mushrooms join the light.
Nature's jests, a merry sound,
In this woodland, joy is found!

The Fabled Heart of the Glade

In the glade, a tale unfolds,
Where laughter mixes with the bold.
A chipmunk's hat, slipped off his head,
The woodland folk all laughed instead!

Pine trees sway with knowing grins,
As the hedgehogs spin like whirly pins.
A blindfolded raccoon's feathery mess,
Is it a game or is it stress?

The fox tells tales of ghostly fright,
While crickets chirp throughout the night.
The whispers roll, 'Now that's the fun!'
As fireflies dance, their work is done.

In this heart of playful cheer,
All creatures bask in their frontier.
With every joke and funny spree,
They find a spark of wild glee!

Timeless Chronicles of the Forest

The trees stand tall, with story yet,
A jester's cap, a silly pet.
A bear in boots, doing a jig,
Swaying offbeat, oh what a gig!

A whisper here, a chuckle there,
Where mushrooms wear the finest flair.
The raccoon sings, with voice so grand,
While squirrels flick acorns in a band.

The sun dips low, a race begins,
With rabbits aiming for the wins.
Their feet a blur, their ears a flop,
In timeless tales, the giggles top!

So gather 'round, with joy you'll see,
These chronicles of glee set free.
From each tall tale, a tickle grows,
In forest chronicles, laughter flows!

Serenades of the Swaying Giants

In the realm of towering trees,
Whispers float upon the breeze.
A sloth sings ballads, slow and sweet,
While woodpeckers join with a steady beat.

The giants sway to every note,
With critters lining up to gloat.
A turtle's dance, oh what a sight,
With rhythm that's close to taking flight!

The winds play tricks, a heady tease,
As brambles tangle, what a sneeze!
A chorus grows with every laugh,
In serenades, they share the craft.

So swing along, join in the jest,
Where nature thrives, it's simply the best.
With every beat and playful whirl,
Swaying giants let laughter unfurl!

A Symphony of Rustling Foliage

In the park where squirrels thrive,
They chatter and they leap, so alive.
Leaves giggle in a breezy jest,
While ants march on, a tiny quest.

Branches swing, a leafy band,
Nature's circus, oh so grand.
A pigeon lands with quite a flair,
"Did you see my aerial air?"

Dandelions dance, in bloom so bold,
Telling tales of secrets told.
The wind whispers to all who pass,
"Join the fun, don't be so crass!"

Under the tree, a picnic spree,
Sandwiches shared, and laughter free.
Juicy fruits make the day complete,
With cheeky ants, quick on their feet.

Songs of the Sylvan Spirit

A raccoon sings, so out of tune,
Moonlit nights, beneath the moon.
Owls join in with wisdom's glare,
While fireflies light up the air.

The brook babbles, a playful tease,
It giggles forth with charming ease.
"Jump in!" it splashes, all so spry,
Yet here I am, just too shy.

Whispers of breeze, with laughter clad,
A ticklish tickle makes us glad.
Each leaf rustles, sharing its tale,
Of mishaps past that never fail.

A critter shows its silly dance,
Bouncing around in a leafy trance.
Nature's choir, all out of sync,
Yet somehow, it makes you wink!

Memories in the Wind

A gust comes by, with tricks to tell,
It sways the branches, oh so well.
Twirling hats from heads they stole,
While laughter swirls, a jovial roll.

The pastimes here, a playful spread,
Like ants' bold plans, or dreams they wed.
Leaves flutter down—what a sight!
Grounded memories take to flight.

The sun peeks out, with a cheeky grin,
As playful shadows start to spin.
"Hey, watch me dance!" the daisies cheer,
While butterflies sip nectar near.

Jokes of the trees, their barks of wit,
In a world where laughter brightly lit.
A breeze carries forth, a hearty jest,
In nature's realm, we feel so blessed!

The Twilight Dance of the Trees

Beneath the glow of dimming light,
Trees shimmy softly, a joyful sight.
Crickets chirp in rhythmic buzz,
As stars peek out, just because.

The willows sway, they twist and flip,
While shadows form a playful trip.
"Come join us here!" the branches shout,
As dusk wraps round, there's never doubt.

Mice make mischief in the grass,
Playing tag with speed, oh so fast.
A hoot from high—a wise old friend,
Saying, "Join in, let's not pretend!"

With every rustle, a secret shared,
In this twilight dance, we're all ensnared.
Laughter lifts, and worries cease,
In this woodsy waltz, we find our peace.

Secrets Beneath the Bark

In the shade, a squirrel plots,
With acorns filled, he laughs a lot.
Whispers swirl in summer's breeze,
Trees giggle as they sway with ease.

Beneath the bark, there's quite a show,
Worms gossip, and beetles glow.
Mysteries held in knots so tight,
"Can you keep my secret? It's quite a fright!"

Fungi dance in colors bright,
Mushroom parties last all night.
The tree trunks lean a little near,
"Let's play hide and seek, my dear!"

Sticks and stones all take their turns,
As nature's child, the laughter burns.
In leafy realms where shadows dart,
Each trunk and twirl hides a funny part.

Resilience of the Rooted

Roots entwined in a comedy,
Tickling soil, digging endlessly.
Each twist and turn, a clumsy feat,
"I can't quite budge, but isn't it sweet?"

Branches wave with silly grace,
Bending low to scratch their face.
"Why stand tall at all," they say,
"When we can play and dance all day?"

A wind chime installed by a crafty jay,
Plays a tune that leads astray.
With every gust, a goofy sound,
The forest floor erupts, profound!

Nature chuckles, a hearty laugh,
As critters pirouette on the path.
In life's dance, they find delight,
Rooted firmly, but taking flight.

Timeless Tracks through Treetops

High above, the branches sway,
Squirrels spy from far away.
"Found a stash!" the magpie sings,
"A treasure trove of funny things!"

Leaves chatter in the morning sun,
"Which acorn will be the one?"
The path they follow, winding slow,
Is laced with giggles, on they go.

Clouds drift by like fluffy sheep,
"Hey, can you catch me? I won't leap!"
Laughter echoes, birds take flight,
In the treetops, all is light.

With each rustling, stories bloom,
Nature's jesters give a room.
Through twigs and giggles, life's a show,
In this green realm, smiles overflow.

In the Presence of Giants

Mighty trunks stretch to the sky,
With leafy crowns that wave and sigh.
"Can you see me?" the fawns shout,
Amidst the giants, there's no doubt.

Funny faces in the bark,
Each one hides a playful spark.
Swaying slowly, they make a scene,
"Look at us, we're evergreen!"

Tales of old in every ring,
Whisper secrets, birds take wing.
With each tickle of the breeze,
They share laughter amidst the trees.

In shadows deep, the humor blooms,
Amongst the giants, joy resumes.
Nature chuckles, so wise and bold,
In their presence, stories unfold.

Spirits of the Ancient Woods

In the woods, the squirrels shout,
"Where's my acorn? Here, no doubt!"
The trees they laugh with sudden glee,
As the breeze dances, wild and free.

Old owl hoots with a wink in his eye,
"I'm wise, you know, but still I fly!"
The branches wave, a funny sight,
As shadows chase the morning light.

A raccoon juggles twigs and leaves,
While chipmunks pull their silly thieves.
The forest hums, a carnival,
Where laughter echoes, trees stand tall.

At twilight's hush, they twirl and spin,
A woodland dance where all join in.
The spirits laugh, a raucous cheer,
In the woods, we shed our fear.

Fragments of the Timbered Past

Once a tree stood proud and grand,
Its shadow stretched across the land.
But now, it laughs at memories,
Of times it swayed with all the bees.

A wooden chair wobbles with glee,
As ghosts recall their jubilee.
They chuckle loud, with creaks and sighs,
"We lived to party, oh, what lies!"

Bushy tails dash through the glade,
In search of nuts and maybe a trade.
"Hey, bark beetle, want to dance?"
The laughter rolls; it's not by chance.

Fragments of laughter in the air,
Remind us not to take a care.
For timbered tales, both tall and true,
Find joy in all the silly through.

Chants of the Tall Ones

The towering giants sway and hum,
Their rhythm makes the critters come.
"Why did the log cross the road?" they caw,
"To prove it could, just look in awe!"

With knotty knees, they jig and prance,
Old roots join in a merry dance.
The woodland creatures gather round,
To hear the tales of laughter sound.

A fox dons leaves for a fancy hat,
And squirrels clamor, "Where's our mat?"
The tall ones chant, a joyful tune,
While shadows stretch beneath the moon.

Their voices mix with rustling leaves,
A chorus that no one believes.
Yet in these woods, the tales persist,
In merry songs, we can't resist.

The Lament of Lost Branches

Oh, lost branches, where did you go?
You once swung high with hopes aglow.
Now they whisper, a gentle sigh,
As critters joke and pass by.

The woodpecker drums a sorrowed beat,
While chipmunks hop on tiny feet.
"Can we glue you back?" they tease and grin,
As giggles echo, a joyful din.

"Remember the days of rustling leaves?
When games were played and no one grieves?"
The branches chuckle from the ground,
"For we were wild, oh but look, we're found!"

So let's not mourn what time has stole,
In laughter, we find a constant scroll.
For in these woods, both near and far,
The spirit shines, our silly star.

The Wood's Gentle Reverberation

In the forest where shadows creep,
The squirrels chirp and play in heaps.
Acorns tumble with a thud,
While rabbits bounce in muddy flood.

Leaves giggle in the summer breeze,
They rustle jokes among the trees.
A snail slides by, quite out of breath,
Chasing whispers of life and death.

Branches sway with a playful spout,
Mice are dancing, without a doubt.
The groundhog slides, a clumsy feat,
He dramatically tumbles, oh what a treat!

So gather 'round this merry show,
Where nature laughs and spirits glow.
Forget your worries, feel the fun,
In the realm where all life runs.

Notes of the Woodland Song

A bird tunes up on a branch so high,
While a chubby raccoon gives it a try.
The trumpet of frogs begins to play,
In quirky rhythms that brighten the day.

Butterflies flutter in a wild trance,
Their wingtips twirl in a floral dance.
A chipmunk hums an off-key tune,
As the dusk brings a dancing moon.

The brook giggles with a splashing grin,
As tadpoles join with a cheeky spin.
Laughter echoes through the leafy hall,
Nature's jam session, for one and all.

So grab your friends and join the song,
In the woodland choir, where all belong.
With giggles and chirps in the growing light,
We'll jam until the stars shine bright.

Embrace of the Grassy Meadow

In a meadow where the wildflowers thrive,
The grasshoppers leap and suddenly dive.
The bees buzz tales of sweetened dreams,
While daydreaming cows plot their schemes.

A picnic blanket, slightly askew,
Full of sandwiches and ants, too!
The size of those critters, oh what a sight,
Marching in line, ready for a bite!

Dandelions laugh as they blow in the air,
While a young boy curls up without a care.
The sun dips low; it's ticklish fun,
As fireflies twinkle, the day is done.

Join the game of this sunny delight,
In a field where giggles take flight.
With joy in every rustling blade,
These moments in nature can't ever fade.

The Pulse of Nature's Heart

The trees, they wobble, like a jolly dance,
The starlings flip in a vital prance.
The fox, so sly, with a playful bark,
Grins at the rabbits, a trip in the park.

From the pond, a splash, it's quite a sight,
A frog leaps high, in sheer delight.
The turtles ponder, slow and wise,
While crickets chirp their midnight cries.

Nature's heart beats in a comical ton,
From lizard races to a snail's slow run.
Each creature's laughter fills the air,
With a joy only the wild can share.

Let's dance along this crazy beat,
As shadows lengthen and creatures meet.
For in this pulse, life's humor's found,
In every chuckle, in every sound.

In the Embrace of the Wild

A squirrel stole my sandwich, oh dear,
He looked so proud, as if he had no fear.
The birds all cackled, what a scene,
While I stood there feeling quite unseen.

A fox jogged by, wearing fancy shoes,
I swear I heard him singing the blues.
As raccoons danced in a conga line,
I began to think, maybe they'd be fine.

A rabbit popped up, with a hat so tall,
Claiming he was the grandest of them all.
Together we laughed, with glee in the breeze,
Nature's circus, crazy as you please.

The trees all chuckled, their leaves did sway,
Encouraging creatures to come out and play.
In the heart of the wild, where laughter soared,
I learned the woods are never ignored.

The Pulse of the Generations

The elders of the woods hold tales so grand,
Like whispers of wisdom from a magical land.
But sometimes their laughter bursts with delight,
When they recall their wild youth, what a sight!

A tree stump told me, as I sat down,
About a raccoon who wore a crown.
The squirrels held court, playing chess with the bees,
While the wise old owl smirked with ease.

The frogs chimed in with a ribbit duet,
Claiming they'd dance at the next sunset.
The chipmunks joined, with a tap and a spin,
In this woodland rave, everyone wins!

And as moonlight danced on leaves so bright,
We shared our giggles under the night.
For in the forest, with laughter and cheer,
Every generation's voice rings loud and clear.

Messenger of the Mellow Woods

A squirrel was sending out text in a rush,
With acorns as emojis, what a fun crush!
The trees leaned in, trying to see,
What mischief awaited, oh, let it be!

The rabbits were gossiping, tails in the air,
Dishing out secrets with a debonair flair.
"Oh, did you hear? Old Badger's a star,
He's hosting a dance party, not too far!"

They hopped and they skipped, all in a line,
With melodies sweet, in a rhythm divine.
But a startled deer jumped, tripping on clover,
A comedic tumble, the laughs took over!

As dusk painted skies in hues of delight,
The woods came alive with joy and pure light.
In this haven of laughter, so warm and good,
I found my heart dancing among the wood.

Wistful Thoughts among the Trees

Once I pondered quietly, under a tree,
About the days gone by, what could they be?
The raccoons chimed in, with a wink and a nod,
"Life's just a romp, go get your mod!"

I watched as the sunbeams splashed all around,
While whispers of trees sang a whimsical sound.
A turtle had tales, slow but so wise,
Of how he outsmarted the cleverest spies.

The grasshoppers jumped, showcasing their skills,
While fireflies sparkled like twinkling thrills.
Together we mused on the mysteries deep,
In a world where humor and magic do leap!

With every leaf rustle, laughter came near,
In this soft sanctuary, nothing to fear.
Wistful and funny, with nature we play,
In the embrace of green, we live day by day.

Fables of the Timbered Crown

In a crown of green, a squirrel does sit,
With acorns as treasures, his wit's quite a hit.
He juggles his finds, a show to behold,
While the rabbits all chuckle at stories retold.

The owl gives a hoot, says, 'You've got the grace!'
But a chipmunk runs by, makes the whole forest race.
The wise and the silly, they all join the fun,
In fables that twinkle beneath the sun.

The deer tell of journeys through shadows and light,
While the hedgehogs all giggle, their spikes snug and tight.
Every tale twists and turns, a laugh is the goal,
In the stories of those who frolic and stroll.

A porcupine sneezes, sends everyone flying,
With laughter and chaos, it's clear none are crying.
In timbered domains, where the wild creatures roam,
They dance through the fables, make the woods feel like home.

Resounding through Leaves

A chipmunk once claimed he could sing like a bird,
But his tunes were so funny, the trees loudly stirred.
The turtles rolled over, the frogs croaked along,
With giggles erupting, they joined in the song.

A breeze caught his voice, it flew far and wide,
Tickling the branches, where laughter would bide.
The wisdom of elders met folly with cheer,
As the forest resounded, it echoed near and clear.

The grasshoppers jumped, doing jig after jig,
While a sleepy old badger just twirled with a twig.
Each note danced with joy, so the winds could all hear,
That not all great legends must fit every ear.

In the grove's busy heart, where the soldier ants march,
Some tomfoolery started, beneath the grand arch.
With a wink to the woodpecker, they giddily weave,
A symphony silly, resounding through leaves.

The Soul of the Shaded Realm

In shadows of giants where giggles play peek,
A wise old raccoon, with a mask, loves to speak.
He shares all his tales of the night and the day,
With a wink in his eye, making mischief his way.

The fireflies flicker, like stars in a spree,
While rabbits debate if it's night or it's sea.
The raccoon just chuckles, says, 'Life's like a game,
Play your part well, and you'll never feel tame.'

A dance on the moss, where the soft shadows glide,
The frogs leap and croak, their ballet filled with pride.
The secrets of night, they twirl through the trees,
Sharing funny stories with the whispers of breeze.

A wisecracking fox offers riddles so bright,
Making all of them ponder till the end of the night.
Each chuckle a treasure, in the realms they unveil,
As the soul of the shaded forever will sail.

Harmonies of the Hidden Grove

In a grove where the laughter blooms bright like a rose,
The mice host a feast, oh, but nobody knows!
The spoons are all tiny, the plates made of leaves,
Yet the giggles echo, making humor believe.

The badgers are chefs, with their clumsy old paws,
They serve up their dishes with no apparent cause.
A recipe fails, but their spirits stay high,
As the squirrels all steal from the stash piled nearby.

With a flick of his tail, a dancer takes flight,
While the owls compete in their dance-off at night.
A chorus of creatures sings tales funny and bold,
In the hidden grove where the best jokes unfold.

The trees sway in rhythm, the leaves softly clap,
As the critters all gather and share in a nap.
Morning brings giggles, a fresh day to start,
In harmonies sweet where the laughter is art.

Silence Between Roots.

In a quiet spot, where the ground is cool,
The worms sit around, playing cards after school.
With laughter they giggle, under a bluesy sky,
While squirrels in tuxedos stand by, oh my!

They bet on the acorns, rolling just right,
While ants throw confetti, it's quite the sight.
A gopher's the dealer, oh what a laugh,
As trees chuckle softly, seeking their half.

Down by the creek, the frogs sing a tune,
While turtles in shades dance to the moon.
The roots, they all wiggle, beneath the earth's crust,
Sharing their secrets, in laughter and trust.

So here in this place, the giggles resound,
With creatures of all sorts, merriment found.
Under their shelter, the fun never halts,
In a world of nature, where joy never fawns.

Whispers Beneath the Canopy

Beneath the green arms, the shadows do play,
A family of owls holds court at the bay.
They hoot and they holler, like old pals in jest,
Telling tall tales, they think they're the best.

A fox named Rick, with a sly little grin,
Claims he once caught a rabbit, but it got away again.
The squirrels are snickering, they know he's a tease,
"Last week you tripped, and fell right on your knees!"

The breeze carries giggles, a rustle so sly,
As leaves whisper gossip, beneath the bright sky.
With laughter, they flutter, in colors so bright,
Creating a symphony, a fantastic sight.

With a wink and a wiggle, the branches they sway,
As critters below play, in a whimsical way.
The world is all merry when nature's in tune,
Beneath the lush canopy that shelters the moon.

Shadows of the Ancient Grove

In the depths of a grove, where shadows abound,
A critter committee meets up all around.
The turtles play poker, their shells shining bright,
While the fireflies flicker, a dazzling light.

An elder tree chuckles, with stories to share,
Of times he was younger, with wild, wondrous flair.
He speaks of the storms, and each triumph and fright,
As the raccoons gather 'round, eyes open wide with delight.

A wise old owl, perched high on a limb,
Winks at the crowd, as the tales start to brim.
"Once, I saw a cat that thought it could sing,
But all it could do was make crows take wing!"

Laughter erupts through the leaves overhead,
As the night air vibrates with stories well said.
In shadows of giants, the fun never fades,
In the heart of the grove, where friendship cascades.

Songs From Twisted Branches

From branches twisted and gnarled, notes do arise,
With the chirps of the birds and the hum of the flies.
A band of raccoons bring out their whole crew,
With tambourines clanging, join in, it's true!

A rabbit beats bongo drums made out of bark,
While badgers play bass lines, adding their spark.
The trees sway along, in rhythm and cheer,
As crickets compose the most charming of tunes here.

The melodies float like the fluff from the breeze,
With charm and with laughter that puts hearts at ease.
They sing of adventures from the morning till dark,
Until sleep gently lulls them, sweet music the arc.

So under the starlight, they party away,
In a symphony woven where night turns to day.
These songs from the branches fill the air with delight,
In the wild woods of wonder, everything feels right.

Chronicles of the Bark

A squirrel with a hat, so quite absurd,
It scurries and leaps, much like a bird.
It steals all the acorns, what a sly chap,
While chatting with crows, he takes a nap.

The winds that whistle, they tickle the leaves,
The bark has heard stories, oh how it grieves!
A raccoon in boots, he dances with flair,
Shaking his tail, without a single care.

Swirling and twirling, the shadows do play,
As branches get tangled, laughing away.
A fox with a grin, she plots with delight,
To steal all the snacks, and feast every night.

But alas, the night falls, with mysteries peek,
The tree just chuckles, what a silly week!
For in this great forest, filled with such glee,
The laughter of nature is wild and free.

Traces of the Timber

A tree with a wig, it sways with such pride,
It's a fashion statement, can't be denied!
With leaves as accessories, vibrant and bold,
Every breeze brings whispers of secrets untold.

The birds in their tuxes, they gather to sing,
A concert at dusk, oh what joy they bring!
The wise old owl rolls his eyes and pretends,
His snoring a tune, where folly never ends.

The winds start to giggle, as branches entwine,
While squirrels on stilts trot the humorous line.
With stashes of nuts, oh what a grand mix,
Running in circles, performing their tricks.

But when shadows stretch, and the sky starts to dark,
The tree holds its breath for a trick and a lark.
Tomorrow they'll clown, with the dawn's rosy hue,
For fun in the forest, it's all about you!

Sighs Through the Saplings

Little saplings whisper, in giggles they sway,
Sharing their secrets, come dusk, come day.
With roots all entangled, they plot little schemes,
To play hide and seek beneath sun's golden beams.

A worm in a party hat slips by with a grin,
As laughter erupts from the branches within.
The butterflies flutter, in chaos and joy,
While one little twig dreams of being a toy.

The brook bubbles over, a phrase it repeats,
"Life's just a game, filled with fun little beats!"
And ants with their sandwiches march in a row,
Planning a picnic, that's sure to steal the show.

But as dusk settles in, with stars bright and clear,
Saplings retire, they feel silly and queer.
They tuck in their laughter, for tomorrow they'll play,
With joy in their hearts, and bright smiles on display.

Reflections in the Bark

A log with a mirror, now that's quite a sight,
It critiques its own bark, oh what a delight!
"Too much humidity makes me quite bland,
I need a good polish, not just any hand."

The frogs gather round, in their shiny best shoes,
Comparing their jumps and debating the news.
A turtle in shades, with a swaggering pace,
Sings ballads of love for his favorite space.

The grass starts to giggle, as shadows all sway,
It's a comedy club, after all, at this play!
An owl in disguise, with a fake mustache,
Peddles jokes to the crowd, they all seem to clash.

But as the moon rises, all starts to unwind,
The mirror-calling log leaves its troubles behind.
For laughter and friendship will conquer the dark,
In the heart of the forest, there's always a spark.

Whispers in the Canopy

Birds gossip high in the trees,
Squirrels plot with some ease.
Branches sway like they've had too much,
Hiccuping leaves with a playful touch.

A raccoon wears a leafy crown,
Chasing shadows round and round.
Laughter dances in the air,
Nature's joke—a funny affair.

Frogs ribbit in funny tones,
Tickling roots with silly groans.
Breezes chuckle in delight,
Playing tag with day and night.

So if you wander in the shade,
Join the fun; don't be afraid.
Nature's circus is always near,
With whispers tickling every ear.

Shadows Beneath the Boughs

In the shadows where we play,
Frogs pretend to be ballet.
Sunlight pokes a funny nose,
Tickling feet as laughter grows.

A wise owl with a droll stare,
Counts the squirrels strutting there.
"Who needs a stage?" he coos with glee,
"Nature's the theater for you and me!"

A bunny jigs in mismatched socks,
While the trees rock to the knocks.
All the leaves shake in laughter,
Echoing joy that's here ever after.

So linger here, enjoy the sight,
Where shadows dance and hearts take flight.
Under boughs, life's quirks abound,
In silliness, the joy is found.

Leaves of Yesterday

Whirling leaves from days gone past,
Plotting ways to have a blast.
Rainy days bring splashes loud,
Muddy footprints make us proud.

A chipmunk orders acorns to go,
While the leaves laugh down below.
"Time for a nap!" one sings with flair,
As winds tickle every hair.

Yesterday's giggles fill the air,
Nature's laughter, everywhere.
Windy whispers play a tune,
Under the watchful gaze of the moon.

So gather round, the tales unfold,
Of squirrely antics, bold and bold.
With leaves that dance, the past feels near,
In this old forest, life is dear.

Muffled Secrets of the Forest

In the woods where secrets play,
Mice share jokes in a merry way.
A deer snickers at a fox's dance,
While shadows chuckle in a trance.

Nestled snug in the bramble bed,
A hedgehog dreams of pies and bread.
"Leave your worries at the door,
Come and laugh till you can't anymore!"

Breezes whisper funny tales,
Of fish who dream of fluffy sails.
Every rustle holds a grin,
In cozy nooks where joy begins.

So take a stroll and light your heart,
Join the fun, take part, take part!
With muffled secrets and chuckled cheer,
In this lively place, all's welcome here.

The Heartbeat of the Grove

In the shade where squirrels play,
A rabbit hops, quite in dismay.
The trees whisper secrets low,
While shadows dance, putting on a show.

Laughter rings among the leaves,
A chipmunk steals, oh how it thieves!
The breeze teases with a tickle,
Nature's stage, it's quite the pickle.

Bubbles of joy from streams nearby,
Fish flash tails as they swim by.
Each branch sways with a silly bend,
The critters laugh, their day to spend.

Time stands still, the sun's a clown,
Tripping over its own golden gown.
As the forest giggles with delight,
Nature's jesters bask in sunlight.

Tales Woven in Twigs

Little birds build nests with flair,
Threads of laughter fill the air.
An owl hoots, but wrong shift too,
Mistaking day for evening's brew.

With acorns scattered everywhere,
Raccoons plot their midnight fair.
A rabbit's dance feels quite absurd,
For even grasshoppers have heard.

Mossy tales spun rich with glee,
From beetles sharing their best tea.
A gust of wind sent leaves to fly,
Shrieks of joy as they wave goodbye.

Branches bend to catch the fun,
Bark giggles, it feels like a pun.
In this gathering of silly sprites,
Nature chuckles through the nights.

Beneath the Silent Watcher

Underneath the ancient tree,
A meeting of the critters be.
Squirrels gossip with much delight,
While frogs croak strategies for the night.

The flowers bloom with vibrant cheer,
Seeing antics that draw near.
A ladybug strikes a pose so grand,
While ants march in a conga band.

Beneath the watchful branches wide,
All the laughter cannot hide.
Worms wiggle with a joke or two,
As chatter grows like morning dew.

With every rustle, wit is born,
In nature's humor, never worn.
Under the boughs where fun aligns,
Life's a stage with no confines.

Reflections in Nature's Mirror

In the pond where ripples play,
A frog croaks in a funny way.
With dragonflies zipping past,
They challenge each other to fly fast.

Ducks waddle with a quirky gait,
Creating shadows that sedate.
A fish pops up, says, "What a joke!"
In this mirror, laughter awoke.

Turtles sunbathe, hats on their shells,
Swapping tales, ringing like bells.
The wind chuckles, plays tricks with leaves,
As nature's sound a clown retrieves.

The sunset wraps with a cheeky grin,
Promising tomorrow's fun to begin.
Reflections shimmer, no solemn shrouds,
Just goofy moments beneath the clouds.

Whispers from the Bark

In the forest where trees like to prattle,
Squirrels gossip, while branches rattle,
A sparrow chuckles, a fox rolls his eyes,
As sunlight dances, and laughter flies.

The wise old oak gives advice quite absurd,
Telling the willows, 'You should have heard!'
A raccoon chuckles, all masked and sly,
While ants march on, thinking they can fly.

The breeze carries tales of the nutty old pine,
Who claims he's the tallest, but that's just a line.
When the wind's blowing hard, they all start to sway,
And dance out their secrets in a leafy ballet.

So when you wander under leafy canopies,
Listen closely for nature's sweet symphonies,
For trees have a humor, if you pause to hear,
The punchlines of nature, so delightfully clear.

An Inspiration of Intertwined Dreams

Beneath the boughs where shadows blend,
Lies a world where dreams happily send,
The owl snores loudly while planning his schemes,
And the rabbits unite, sharing their dreams.

The snails plot a race at the edge of the path,
While toads hop around, they're crafting their math,
A turtle, quite wise, takes his sweet, slow time,
Saying, 'Patience is key, it's simply sublime!'

The chirping of crickets sets up quite a show,
As fireflies twinkle, putting on their glow,
In this whimsical dance, each creature takes part,
Chasing moonbeams where laughter can start.

So gather your dreams when you wander this way,
In the land of the odd, where the silly animals play,
The branches will whisper, and joy will delight,
In a tapestry woven of dreams every night.

The Legacy of Leaf and Limb

Upon a branch where the sunbeams peek,
Stands an acorn with victories quite unique,
He brags to the leaves of the sprightly wild,
Of how he grew tall, oh so very mild.

The twigs murmur stories of days gone by,
When a crow learned to dance, oh my, oh my!
With every odd movement, the audience gasped,
As laughter erupted, and stories clasped.

The breeze tells tall tales of a mighty old tree,
Who wore hats made of moss, quite stylish, you see,
With bark as his armor and roots like his shoes,
He strutted through forests with nothing to lose.

So when you pass by, give a chuckle or grin,
For nature's a jokester, without and within,
In this legacy grand, with each leaf and limb,
You'll find joy and laughter, and life's playful whim.

Cadence of the Natural World

In the heart of the woods, where the wild things play,
The rhythm of nature starts to sway,
With critters all dancing to the tree trunk beat,
A symphony played by the earth at your feet.

Frogs croak in tune, while the crickets all sing,
An orchestra vibrant, on no given spring,
The flowers all giggle, their petals agleam,
As the sun sprinkles laughter, it's nature's grand dream.

The badger set out with a step quite absurd,
Tumbling and tripping, oh have you heard?
While the owls keep time with their wise, sleepy hoots,
And the wise old tree sports its leafy green boots.

So step to the tempo of wild woodland cheer,
Let the playful surroundings draw you near,
For in this grand concert, life finds a way,
To blend joy and whimsy in nature's ballet.

www.ingramcontent.com/pod-product-compliance
Lightning Source LLC
Chambersburg PA
CBHW071840160426
43209CB00003B/363